THE SOFT BLACK STARS

Matthew Buckley Smith

Rattle | Studio City, California | 2026

The Soft Black Stars
Copyright © 2026 by Matthew Buckley Smith

All rights reserved

Layout and design by Timothy Green

Cover and design by Daniel Alexander Smith

ISBN: 978-1-931307-64-2

First edition

Rattle Foundation
12411 Ventura Blvd
Studio City, CA 91604
www.rattle.com

The Rattle Foundation is an independent 501(c)3 nonprofit, whose mission is to promote the practice of poetry, and which is not affiliated with any other organization. All poems are works of the imagination. While the perceptions and insights are based on the author's experience, no reference to any real person is intended or should be inferred.

Contents

Acknowledgments	4
Sonnet for My Daughters	11
Stay-at-Home	12
My Lord You	13
The Wife	14
The Seafarer	15
Meditations	17
Spontaneous Loss	18
The Soft Black Stars	19
To His Heart	20
Melancholia	21
To Marilyn Manson	22
Exes	23
Autofiction	24
Motherhood	25
Fatherhood	27
What Work Is	28
Lines on His 42nd Birthday	29
Where the Wild Things Are	30
About the Author	31

Acknowledgments

Thanks to the editors of the following magazines, where poems in this collection first appeared, sometimes in different forms.

32 Poems: "The Soft Black Stars"
Able Muse Review: "Where the Wild Things Are"
Blood Rag: "Sonnet for My Daughters"
First Things: "Spontaneous Loss"
Masculinity: An Anthology of Modern Voices: "Motherhood"
The Nation: "Stay-at-Home"
The New Stylus: "Autofiction" and "Exes"
New Verse Review: "To Marilyn Manson"
Ploughshares: "Melancholia"
Poetry London: "Lines on His 42nd Birthday"
Root Quarterly: "My Lord You"
Smartish Pace: "To His Heart" and "Meditations"
Southern Poetry Review: "Fatherhood" and "The Wife"

Thanks also to the many friends who helped bring this chapbook about—especially Ryan Wilson, to whom two of these excruciatingly personal poems are dedicated. I'll give you all a proper thanks in the next proper book. For now, you know who you are, and I love you.

THE SOFT BLACK STARS

for Joanna
first reader, favorite wife

Turning over the photo Spence read aloud the following inscription: "The little man is so much littler these days. Soon he will know about the soft black stars. And your payment is past due."
   —*Thomas Ligotti, "Teatro Grottesco"*

Sonnet for My Daughters

Tucking you in at night I sometimes think
Of what a piece of shit I used to be,
Of the girls I drove to dinner and to drink,
Whose dads were once pieces of shit like me,
The dads they hugged and left home and defied
In the backseat of my '98 Passat,
While the old men, knowing how well their daughters lied,
Watched hair plug ads and thought and thought and thought,
And later, when everybody was asleep,
Those girls I thought were mine would sneak back in,
Sometimes to call their friends, sometimes to weep,
Sometimes to never think of me again,
But rather of how they'd soon be moving out
For good, those girls I sometimes think about.

Stay-at-Home

Something is always broken in the house—
The dryer vent, the smoke alarm, the range,
A glue trap with a not-quite-murdered mouse,
The coffee pot, a bulb that needs a change.
I right some wrongs, and others I put off.
I clean, I exercise, I take a nap.
The kids need picking up. One has a cough,
The other watches TV in my lap.
We're out of pita bread, we're out of soap.
I might walk to the market, I might not.
Bedtime grows later. There is always hope
For sex if we're not tired. We're tired a lot.
My wife works hard. I do the best I can.
No one who looks at me can see a man.

My Lord You

> *At fourteen I married My Lord you ...*
> —Ezra Pound, "The River-Merchant's
> Wife: A Letter"

I was still a girl when you took me to wife
And gave me everything I thought I wanted.

I loved you, and I learned to love your life;
I was a ghost, and you were all I haunted.

I warmed your bed and bore you healthy sons
And filled your lovely house with lovely things.

Time ran from us the way a river runs
And stung the way a river serpent stings.

For years you were your work, and I was you,
Our boys turned into men, and turned away,

Our house grew still, your reputation grew,
My girlish beauty lessened by the day.

Sometimes in bed, before the light had broken,
I'd watch you sleep and wish we'd never spoken.

The Wife

I thought I'd let you know I read your book.
I ordered it the day I learned your name,

Scrolling through pictures friends and family took
Over some twenty years. You look the same

As in your author photo, more or less—
Your face here thinner, there your straight hair curled,

Your teeth now whitened, as if to impress
Your partners in the corporate healthcare world

To which you bring the promise you once brought
To the cautious poems I took to bed tonight,

While elsewhere, that same man with whom you bought
Your pretty house is stepping off a flight

Into Pacific Standard Time to find
The mother of my children in a bar

Brimming with chummy strangers who don't mind
Their missing rings, or wonder where we are.

The Seafarer

for R.

> *Maeg ic be me sylfum   soðgied wrecan*
> —*"The Seafarer"*

This morning
when you look outside
   it's gone.
You make some coffee,
   take the kids to school,
come back to find
   a paper on the lawn,
and drown the morning,
   waiting like a fool
for something that
   was never really there,
or if it was,
   then only in a dream—
a whiff of salt,
   a horizontal glare—
distractions
   insufficient to redeem
a life devoted, mostly,
   to the waste
of youth, of strength,
   of money, and of hope,
of chasing what
   far better men
have chased,
   and given up,
and, unable to cope
   with failure, tried
in vain to chase again,

[…]

    like you, who can't
remember how it looks,
    that sea
before which you've forever been
    as helpless as
the heroes in your books.

Meditations

They tell us that it's better not to know,
The Romans and the Greeks, too much about
The days that lie ahead, better to go
In darkness as the gentle tug of doubt
Unravels our presentiments, instead
Of being brought to earth by clarity
Or sickened by the deep foreshocks of dread.
Better to stumble backwards than to see.

Picture them: taking breakfast by the sea
As sailboats shuttle plague across the water;
Or kneeling to some civic deity
Though hordes outside the gates prepare for slaughter;
Or in the market, gossiping and joking,
While overhead the mountain goes on smoking.

Spontaneous Loss

Those early weeks, you could have been anyone,
   Too young for fingerprints, much less a name,
And years away from our first catch-and-toss—
   A little flesh and blood, no brain, no bone,
     No one to blame.
You did not count, you were not even close.

We do our best, over breakfast, over work,
   To go back to the way things were before,
The way things never technically were not,
   And we do. We're fine. You left no lasting mark
     We can't ignore,
Just a small stain on the downstairs bathroom grout

That one bad day—the sudden blood, the panic,
   The clotted towels, the cramped emergency room.
Then we were alone again, more living proof
   That this is nature's way, a swift, hygienic
     Numbers game,
Which gives us all we need. Which is not enough.

The Soft Black Stars

The trouble was, you fell in love with him.
Foolhardy, but not hard to understand.
You traded jokes, and drafts, and writing tips—

This painful cut, that poignant synonym.
He finally retired his ampersand.
You learned to say "ellipsis," not "ellipse."

As pen pals you were perfect, or almost.
You liked the way he made you feel as young
As when we met. You liked the way his life

Was nailed down halfway to the other coast.
You told me—and it hardly even stung,
Because I knew, because he had a wife.

In time, of course, the conference weekend came.
You asked for my permission, and I gave it.
What happened that first night I only heard

When you got home. You seemed almost the same,
But something had been lost. You couldn't save it.
Since then, your friend, he hasn't said a word.

To His Heart

for R.

> *Non val cosa nessuna*
> *i moto tuoi, né di sospiri è degna*
> *la terra.*
>   —Giacomo Leopardi, "A se stesso"

Forty-one years is long enough, old heart.
That you are tired, that you will always be

A fragile, limping, elementary
Part of myself from which I cannot part,

That you still love the same insipid lie
Your peers all ceased in childhood to believe,

That, even now, you're trying to retrieve
The doggish hope that you will never die,

That you have kept the time too long already,
That there is little left for which to beat,

That life is no more bitter in defeat
Than it is bored in triumph, that the steady

Pulse you've carried all these years amounts
To nothing in the end but aimless patter—

Take comfort knowing that it doesn't matter.
None of this matters. No, none of this counts.

Melancholia

Before your birth,
   I marked you as my own,
the way I marked
   your mother before hers.
Inscribed on every
   cell of every bone,
the standard of my family
   never blurs.
I coil between the
   makings of your bed,
and in the small hours
   whisper you awake.
I poison every
   sentence in your head,
and all those comforts
   other people take.
Eat salmon, buy a doodle,
   down the pills
the doctor tenders you
   illegibly,
quit drinking,
   join a gym with all the frills,
become the man
   you've always meant to be ...
Try as you might,
   you'll never quite forget
what crouches in
   the corners of your mind.
Hope is a word. I am
   the alphabet.
Some gods are real, but
   not the loving kind.

To Marilyn Manson

You might be why
I didn't kill myself
   some night in '98 or '99.
A Southern Catholic atheist
   yourself, you had a voice
I took back then for mine.
   You soured, and I survived,
for good or ill, depending
   on the day, I can't decide.
I'm over both your music
   and the hill, and out
of arguments for suicide.
   Meanwhile, I've learned
the vicious metaphor
   I took you for was
no figure of speech.
   Nor, it seems, are you
Southern, Catholic, or
   anyone with anything
to teach. And yet, for me,
   those early records stand
apart. Somehow I thought
   you'd understand.

Exes

Renée was just a way
of getting back
some savor of the girl

who came before,
the one who was
supposed to seal

the crack left
by the one you left
in Baltimore,

who needed most nights
half a dozen beers
before she'd drop by yours

at half past two
to show off
what she'd picked up

in the years
since losing
the original of you.

Autofiction

Last night in bed she asked for something new,
And being the enlightened types we are,
She'd already mentioned trying it with you
That night you finally met up at the bar,
Having for twelve dry months made do with text,
And wincing author photos, and the chance
That from one tipsy conference to the next
Your lyrical flirtations might advance
To richly drafted novelistic pages
Set in a suitably rundown hotel,
Where writers of all qualities and ages
Enacted stories they might someday sell.
Then, having left your cum in her, you sent
My wife a final one-line farewell note,
And blocked her on the internet, and went
Silent for your own sake. Meanwhile she wrote
A story all about your sad affair,
For which she'd win not one but several prizes
And endless praise for her "unflinching stare"
And "pitiless deployment" of surprises
By which your dashing stand-in is redeemed
Until the denouement, when he is not,
Being no more than what he always seemed,
An average prick, brought in to spur the plot,
Which finds, at last, our heroine alone,
Between Zoom calls, the workweek halfway through,
Suppressing a desire to see her phone
Light up once more with lovely words from you.

Motherhood

> *That night in the field, all the eggs basketed inside me*
> *lay down with me when I lay down*
> *next to the man who would not*
> *be the father of my daughters ...*
>   —Cecily Parks, "Motherhood"

You came home tipsy from a girls' night out
    And read me a poem you'd found while scrolling Twitter—
        As one of your friends was going on about
            Her husband's weakness for the babysitter.

You loved this poem, though you were afraid to show it,
    And not because ten years ago you swore
        You hated reading poems, and being a poet,
            And just could not be bothered anymore,

And not because while you were with your girls,
    I was convincing ours to go to bed,
        Their teeth swiped clean, a comb run through their curls,
            Their foreheads kissed, their favorite stories read,

But maybe because it was a poem of love,
    And not for the man the poet was married to,
        Nor for the girls she was the mother of,
            But for the cad who'd slept with her in lieu

Of his own much-loved, much-wronged, much-offstage wife,
    A wife he'd never truly meant to leave,
        Any more than he'd meant his talk of a new life,
            Despite the young poet's longing to believe,

[...]

And maybe because this poem for a married man
    Was a surrogate for the poem you would not write,
        About a different, likewise married man,
            On a different, likewise unencumbered night,

And because, although the title of this poem
    Was "Motherhood," it mentioned terms like *mother*
        And *children* and *father* and *marriage* and *homelife* and *home*
        Scarcely at all, in favor of another

More urgent and enthralling set of words,
    Words like *yes*, *stranger*, *craving*, *touch*, and *youth*,
        In lines that swooned with flowers and beasts and birds
            And sounded, to your sick heart, like the truth.

Fatherhood

All of the children disappear.
It happens like a fairytale,
This thing you never thought to fear.
All of the children disappear.
As inch by inch and year by year
Your efforts to protect them fail.
All of the children disappear.
It happens like a fairytale.

What Work Is

> *You know what work is—if you're*
> *old enough to read this you know what*
> *work is, although you may not do it.*
> *—Philip Levine, "What Work Is"*

The parents of my parents' parents' parents
Sold furniture and legal expertise
And counted out their fortunes by the hour,
Neglecting passion, pleasure, and appearance
                For the makeshift peace
That comes with seeing one's name above the door.

They purchased, invoiced, supervised, and signed,
And seldom gave a second thought to luck,
But filled their Frigidaires and bassinets
And left a thriving enterprise behind,
                Of which the stock
Muddies my conscience while it clears my debts.

Meanwhile, I bathe and feed my daughters, who—
Although they've learned the words for *work* and *earn*—
Are years from knowing either what they mean
Or which distracted parent of their two
                Our tax return
Considers a productive citizen.

And this small thing I think of as my work,
This homely piecemeal borrowing of words,
Does nothing, and has not to date diminished
The price of every business hour I shirk,
                And its rewards
Are long delinquent, and it's never, never finished.

Lines on His 42nd Birthday

It's harder, at an age like this, to say
Just how your dreams would look if they came true,
After so many decades of delay,
Of watching younger dreamers learn from you
Which choices to avoid as they dreamed on
More cleverly than you did, who still dream
Of something better, still awake at dawn,
Shutting your eyes against the first hot beam
The day sends, not for you but for your wife,
The one who's lapped you by a whole career,
The one you'd still want in another life,
A life in which it daily grows less clear
Just what would differ from the life you know:
Not wife, not kids, not family, friends, or dogs,
Not anything that you might own or owe,
Except the downstairs sink, which always clogs,
And five more bookcases, or maybe six,
Perhaps a painting for the landing wall,
But otherwise, the dream that really sticks
Concerns yourself, about which you'd change all—
A tear-down, better totaled than repaired,
You'd see yourself made over from the start,
A sounder body, with a brain that dared
To dream less, and a wholly different heart.

Where the Wild Things Are

In the book our daughters love,
    dark thickets spring
up from the floor to claim
    young Max's room,
supplanting every
    pale familiar thing
with starlit branch and stamen,
    stalk and bloom.
So when you set the white
    noise app to play
its loop of *Forest Sounds*
    on a Summer Night,
and shut the blinds,
    and strip, and shyly say
you wouldn't mind
    if I turned out the light,
I wonder if our girls upstairs
    might hear
the savage noises
    coming from beneath,
and think again of
    Max's friends, and fear
once more the terrible
    eyes and claws and teeth,
and whether they'd be
    any less afraid
to learn these were the woods
    where they were made.

About the Author

MATTHEW BUCKLEY SMITH is the author of *Midlife* (Measure, 2024) and *Dirge for an Imaginary World* (Able Muse, 2012). His poems have been featured in *American Life in Poetry*, *Best American Poetry*, and *Poetry Daily*. He hosts the poetry podcast *SLEERICKETS*.

matthewbuckleysmith.com

About the Rattle Chapbook Series

The Rattle Chapbook Series publishes and distributes a chapbook to all of *Rattle*'s print subscribers along with each quarterly issue of the magazine. Most selections are made through the annual Rattle Chapbook Prize competition (deadline: January 15th). For more information, and to order other chapbooks from the series, visit our website.

2026 | *The Soft Black Stars* by Matthew Buckley Smith
2025 | *no matter how it ends a bluebird's song* by Kat Lehmann
        Haunt Me by José Enrique Medina
        Backlit by Liz Robbins
2024 | *Cheap Motels of My Youth* by George Bilgere
        In Which by Denise Duhamel
        Sky Mall by Eric Kocher
2023 | *The Fight Journal* by John W. Evans
        At the Car Wash by Arthur Russell
        Plucked by Miracle Thornton
2022 | *Imago, Dei* by Elizabeth Johnston Ambrose
        The Morning You Saw a Train of Stars … by CooXooEii Black
        Visiting Her in Queens Is More Enlightening … by Michael Mark
2021 | *The Death of a Migrant Worker* by Gil Arzola
        A Plumber's Guide to Light by Jesse Bertron
        I Will Pass Even to Acheron by Amanda Newell
2020 | *Adjusting to the Lights* by Tom C. Hunley
        A Juror Must Fold in on Herself by Kathleen McClung
        Falling off the Empire State Building by Jimmy Pappas
2019 | *The Last Mastodon* by Christina Olson
        Hansel and Gretel Get the Word on the Street by Al Ortolani
        Did You Know? by Elizabeth S. Wolf
2018 | *To Those Who Were Our First Gods* by Nickole Brown
        Tales From the House of Vasquez by Raquel Vasquez Gilliland
        Punishment by Nancy Miller Gomez
        A Bag of Hands by Mather Schneider
2017 | *In America* by Diana Goetsch
        The Whetting Stone by Taylor Mali

www.**Rattle**.com